Minnesota

by the Capstone Press
Geography Department

Reading Consultant:
William E. Lass
Professor of History
Mankato State University

CAPSTONE PRESS
MANKATO, MINNESOTA

C A P S T O N E   P R E S S
818 North Willow Street • Mankato, Minnesota 56001

Library of Congress Cataloging-in-Publication Data
    Minnesota/by the Capstone Press Geography Department
    p. cm.--(One Nation)
    Includes bibliographical references and index.
    Summary: Gives an overview of the state of Minnesota, including its
    history, geography, people, and living conditions.
    ISBN 1-56065-500-3
    1. Minnesota--Juvenile literature. [1. Minnesota.]
    I. Capstone Press. Geography Dept. II. Series.
F606.3.M56 1997
977.6--dc21
                                            96-46870
                                               CIP
                                                AC

Photo credits
Gary Alan Nelson, cover, 5 (right), 16, 18, 28, 34
Flag Research Center, 4 (left)
Sage Productions/James Sneddon, 4 (right)
FPG/Larry West, 5 (left); Richard Smith, 10; James
    Randklev, 12; Tom Carroll, 26; David McGlynn, 30;
    Gail Shumway, 32
Northfield Historical Society, 6, 8
Peter Ford, 21
James P. Rowan, 22
Paula Borchardt, 25

Table of Contents

Fast Facts about Minnesota

State Flag

Location: In the Upper Midwest region of north central United States

Size: 86,943 square miles (226,052 square kilometers)

Population: 4,517,416 (1993 United States Census Bureau figures)

Capital: St. Paul

Date admitted to the Union: May 11, 1858; the 32nd state

Common loon

Largest cities: Minneapolis, St. Paul, Bloomington, Duluth, Rochester, Brooklyn Park, Coon Rapids, Burnsville, Plymouth, St. Cloud

Nicknames: The Gopher State; The North Star State

State bird: Common loon

State flower: Pink and white lady's slipper

Pink and white lady's slipper

State tree: Norway pine

State song: *"Hail! Minnesota"* by Truman E. Rickard and Arthur E. Upson

Norway pine

5

Chapter 1
The Northfield Raid

It was a sunny afternoon. The James/Younger gang headed toward Northfield, Minnesota. The eight men had planned to rob the First National Bank. Three of the men went inside the bank. The others waited.

But the robbers could not open the safe. They started shooting up the town. Two townspeople fell to the ground.

Merchants from nearby stores fired back. They killed two robbers and wounded five. The gang galloped out of town. From start to finish, the raid lasted seven minutes. This happened on September 7, 1876.

Every year, citizens of Northfield reenact the bank raid.

Only Jesse James (left) and Frank James escaped the unsuccessful Northfield First National Bank holdup.

Later, a posse went after the gang. A posse is a group of citizens organized to catch a criminal. They captured three and killed one. Only Jesse James and Frank James escaped.

Northfield Today

Every September, the people of Northfield reenact the raid. Men and women wear clothes from the 1870s. Actors ride into town. They draw their guns. A reenactment of the shoot-out blazes at the First National Bank. Townspeople and visitors watch from the sidewalk.

Today, Northfield is known as a college town. St. Olaf College is west of the downtown area. Carleton College is to the northeast.

Minnesota's Many Attractions

Minnesota is called the Land of 10,000 Lakes. Minnesotans can fish, boat, and swim. Water skiing was first done on Lake Pepin.

Minnesotans also enjoy winter sports. Many go snowmobiling, skiing, ice skating, and ice fishing. Snowmobiles were invented in Minnesota.

Minnesota is home to the United States Hockey Hall of Fame. It is located in the city of Eveleth on Hat Trick Avenue.

For indoor fun, Minnesotans enjoy the Mall of America. It is in Bloomington, a suburb of Minneapolis. This mall is one of the largest in North America. It has more than 500 stores. It also has an amusement park and a walk-through aquarium.

Chapter 2
The Land

Minnesota lies in the north central United States. Four other midwestern states are its neighbors. They are Wisconsin, Iowa, South Dakota, and North Dakota.

North of Minnesota is Canada. Lake Superior touches northeastern Minnesota.

The Superior Upland
Rugged, rocky land covers most of northern Minnesota. This area is called the Superior Upland. Large lakes dot the area. There are also many forests. Large iron ore deposits lie under the land.

Minnesota's land has many lakes and forests.

Rugged cliffs line the Minnesota shores of Lake Superior.

Minnesota's northeastern tip is called the Arrowhead. Rugged cliffs line the shores of Lake Superior. To the north is the Canadian border. Lakes and rivers form the border.

Eagle Mountain is in the Arrowhead. It reaches 2,301 feet (690 meters) above sea level. This is Minnesota's highest point.

Minnesota's lowest point is also in the Arrowhead. It is along Lake Superior. This point is 602 feet (181 meters) above sea level.

Minnesota has the northernmost point of the continental United States. The continental United States is the 48 states not including Hawaii and Alaska. Minnesota is called the North Star State because of this northernmost point. The waters of Lake of the Woods cover it.

South of Lake of the Woods is Red Lake. This is the largest lake within Minnesota.

The Drift Plains

The Drift Plains are west and south of the Upland. Large sheets of ice called glaciers smoothed this land. Some of the nation's best farmland is in the Drift Plains.

The Red River flows north through the western plains. The river forms Minnesota's border with North Dakota.

The Minnesota River cuts across the prairie in the south. At Mankato, it turns north. It empties into the Mississippi River near Minneapolis.

The Mississippi Valley

The Mississippi River starts in northern Minnesota. Its source is Lake Itasca. It flows south to Minneapolis and St. Paul.

East of St. Paul, the St. Croix River joins the Mississippi. These two rivers form part of Minnesota's southeastern border with Wisconsin. The Mississippi continues past Minnesota and flows through many other states. It ends in the Gulf of Mexico.

Southern Minnesota

Minnesota's southeastern tip has steep hills. Here, fast-flowing streams have cut valleys.

The state's southwestern corner has level land. Farmers there raise grain and livestock.

Climate

Minnesota's winters are long and cold. International Falls is known as the coldest place in the nation. The city is located on Minnesota's northern border with Ontario. Blizzards bring ice and snow across the state. During the winter, about 70 inches (178 centimeters) of snow fall along Lake Superior.

Summers are warm and humid. Humid means the air is heavy with moisture. Storms cross the state in spring and summer. They bring lightning, hail, and tornadoes.

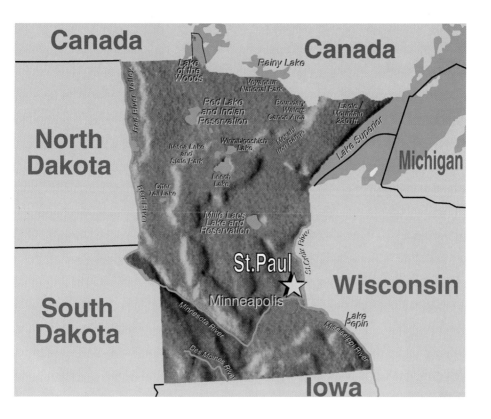

Wildlife

Bear, moose, and timber wolves live in Minnesota's northern forests. Deer are found throughout the state. Pheasants and partridges nest in southern prairies.

Game fish swim in Minnesota's lakes and rivers. They include walleye, trout, and northern pike.

Chapter 3
The People

Most Minnesotans live in the southeastern part of the state. The Twin Cities area is also heavily populated. About 55 percent of Minnesota's population lives there.

The state's population is growing. In the early 1990s, it grew by almost 5 percent. This was the Midwest's fastest growth rate.

European Ethnic Groups

Almost 95 percent of Minnesotans have European or Canadian backgrounds. They descended from European and Canadian immigrants. Immigrants are people who come to another country to settle.

The Twin Cities has 55 percent of Minnesota's population.

17

Norwegian immigrants started farms in southern Minnesota because the land reminded them of home.

Minnesota's first settlers came from eastern states. They included New Englanders and New Yorkers. Others arrived from Ohio, Illinois, Michigan, and Wisconsin. Their families had come earlier from Europe.

In the 1850s, many people came directly from northern and western Europe. German farmers settled near New Ulm in 1856. St. Paul had a large Irish population.

Swedish immigrants settled north of St. Paul. Norwegians started farms in southern Minnesota. The state's land and climate reminded them of home.

In the 1890s, immigrants arrived from eastern and southern Europe. They came from Italy, Poland, Yugoslavia, and Russia. Most of them worked in Minnesota's iron mines.

Some people also moved to Minnesota from Canada. Some groups of French Canadians still live in the Red River Valley.

Today, German Americans make up Minnesota's largest ethnic group. An ethnic group is people with a common culture.

African Americans

Minnesota's first African Americans were fur traders. This was in the early 1800s. Many African Americans moved to Minnesota in the 1940s. They wanted jobs in factories.

Today, about 2 percent of Minnesotans are African American. Minneapolis, St. Paul, and Duluth have large African-American communities.

Asian Americans

Almost 2 percent of Minnesotans have Asian-American backgrounds. About 18,000 Hmong live in the state. They are Minnesota's largest Asian group. The Hmong came from northern Laos in the 1980s. Most of them live in the Twin Cities.

Minnesota has other Asian-American groups. They include people from Korea, China, India, and Vietnam.

Many Asian Americans work in Minnesota's high-tech industries. Others own shops and restaurants.

Hispanic Americans

A little more than 1 percent of Minnesotans have Hispanic backgrounds. Most came from Mexico, Puerto Rico, Colombia, or Cuba. Many Hispanics live in Minnesota's cities.

Native Americans

About 50,000 Native Americans live in Minnesota. They are Dakota and Ojibwa.

Many Native Americans live in Minnesota's cities. Others live on reservations. A reservation is land set aside for use by Native

The Minnesota Ojibwa hold powwows at Hinckley.

Americans. There are 11 reservations in
Minnesota. Red Lake and White Earth are large
Ojibwa reservations. They are in northern
Minnesota. Dakota reservations are in southern
Minnesota.

Each reservation in Minnesota has a place to
gamble called a casino. The casinos provide a
lot of money for the reservations. Some
reservations have built new schools. Others
now have health-care centers.

Chapter 4
Minnesota History

The first people reached Minnesota about 12,000 years ago. About 1,500 years ago, mound builders were in Minnesota. They shaped some mounds to look like animals.

In the 1600s, Native Americans lived in northeastern Minnesota. These were the Dakota and Ojibwa. Fighting broke out between the two groups. The Dakota moved into southern Minnesota.

French Traders and Explorers

French fur traders arrived in 1660. They traveled from Canada. They traded with the

French fur traders called voyageurs traveled through Minnesota by canoe.

Native Americans. The traders exchanged guns and knives for furs.

In 1679, Daniel Greysolon, sieur Duluth, entered Minnesota. This was near present-day Duluth. He claimed Minnesota for France.

In 1680, Father Louis Hennepin traveled the Mississippi River. He named the St. Anthony Falls. It is now located near present-day Minneapolis.

Three Nations in Minnesota

By 1732, England had 13 colonies. They were along the Atlantic Ocean. England also wanted France's lands to the west.

England gained some French lands in 1763. They were east of the Mississippi River and included northeastern Minnesota.

In 1783, the 13 English colonies won their independence. England lost its land east of the Mississippi. That land became part of the United States.

In 1803, the United States bought land from France. This was called the Louisiana Purchase. The land was west of the

The United States Army built Fort Snelling in the 1820s.
People can still visit it today.

Mississippi. All of Minnesota was now in the
United States.

Moving to Minnesota

The United States Army built Fort Snelling in
the 1820s. This fort helped the United States
control the Mississippi Valley area. The fort sat
where the Minnesota River joined the
Mississippi.

Loggers and farmers moved into Minnesota. Sawmills went up along the St. Croix River. Flour mills were built at St. Anthony Falls.

Treaties and the Dakota Uprising

In the 1850s, Minnesota's Native Americans signed away their lands. They moved to reservations. The U.S. government promised to help the Native Americans by sending food.

Farmers moved onto Dakota lands. Logging companies moved into Ojibwa forests.

In 1862, the Dakota received no food from the government. Many of them starved. The Dakota killed about 500 settlers because the government had broken their promise to send food.

Minnesotans and government troops ended the uprising with military force. They hanged 38 Dakota leaders in Mankato.

Growth of a New State

Meanwhile, Minnesota became the 32nd state. On May 11, 1858, Minnesota entered the Union. St. Paul was the state capital.

Minnesota grew quickly. Wheat farms started in southern Minnesota. More flour mills were

St. Paul is Minnesota's state capital.

Duluth became a great port city. Ships filled with goods entered and left its harbors.

built near St. Anthony Falls. The city of Minneapolis grew around the falls. Iron ore was shipped from northeastern Minnesota.

Duluth became a great port city. Ships left Duluth carrying lumber, grain, and iron ore.

The Early 1900s

During World War I (1914-1918), Minnesota helped the war effort. The state's iron ore went to defense factories. Minnesota wheat fed the troops.

28

In 1918, Minnesotans formed the Farmer-Labor party. The party worked to help farmers and factory workers.

Then the Great Depression (1929-1939) hit the United States. Mines and factories closed. Workers lost their jobs. The price of farm crops fell.

Minnesota had its first Farmer-Labor governor from 1931 to 1936. Governor Floyd Olson helped Minnesotans keep their farms. He took steps to help the jobless.

In 1941, the United States entered World War II (1939-1945). Minnesota factories made parts for airplanes and ships.

Recent Changes

Manufacturing changed after the war. New factories made electronic equipment. Minneapolis and St. Paul attracted computer companies.

Minnesota's government brought changes, too. In 1987, the school-choice program started. Families could choose which schools their children would attend.

In 1992, Minnesota started HealthRight. This program gave poor and jobless people health insurance. It is now called Minnesota Care.

Chapter 5
Minnesota Business

Agriculture and mining industries helped build Minnesota. Manufacturing is now Minnesota's largest business.

Minnesota also has a large service industry. Minneapolis is a banking and insurance center. Tourism and trade are other service industries.

Agriculture

Corn and soybeans are Minnesota's leading crops. The Red River Valley has large wheat farms. Sugar beets and potatoes grow there, too.

Dairy cattle are Minnesota's most important livestock. Hogs and turkeys are other livestock.

Tourism and service industries are big Minnesota businesses. The Mall of America has many tourists and many employees.

Some Minnesota farmers raise interesting animals such as these wooly llamas.

Minnesota's chickens lay many eggs. Some farmers also raise emus, ostriches, and llamas.

Manufacturing

Food products lead Minnesota's manufacturing efforts. General Mills, Pillsbury, and Hormel are headquartered in the state.

Flour, cake mixes, and cereals are leading products. Meat packing and canning take place throughout the state. Large amounts of butter and cheese are made in Minnesota, too. The Red River Valley has sugar refineries.

Factories in Minneapolis, St. Paul, and Rochester make computers. Farm machinery is also made in Minnesota.

Chemicals and paper are other Minnesota products. Companies in Minneapolis and Mankato publish books.

Mining

Minnesota leads the states in mining iron ore. Today, this is a low grade of ore called taconite.

Granite comes from central Minnesota. Southern Minnesota has deposits of limestone.

Service Industries

Minnesota has many visitors each year. These people stay at resorts and hotels. They eat in restaurants. Tourism earns Minnesota about $11 billion each year.

Trade is another important Minnesota service business. Super Valu is one of the nation's leading grocery chains. It is based in the Twin Cities. The department store Dayton Hudson has headquarters there, too. This company also owns Target and Marshall Field's.

Chapter 6
Seeing the Sights

Minnesota license plates say "Land of 10,000 Lakes." The state really has more than 15,000 freshwater lakes. Parks and museums also draw many visitors. Outdoors and indoors, Minnesota has much to offer.

Voyageur Country
Voyageurs National Park is on the Minnesota-Canada border. The park has more than 30 lakes. Visitors can trace the path of voyageurs. Voyageurs were French fur traders. They traveled through Canada and Minnesota by canoe.

The Boundary Waters Canoe Area is one of the many beautiful sights to see in Minnesota.

The Boundary Waters Canoe Area (BWCA) is east of the park. It covers 1 million acres (404,700 hectares). People paddle canoes over its several thousand lakes.

Ely is to the south of the Boundary Waters area. Campers pick up supplies in this town. Then they head north with their canoes.

Arrowhead Country

Grand Portage National Monument is on Lake Superior. It is at Minnesota's northeastern tip. Grand Portage was an important 1700s trading post. Today, the post has been rebuilt. Visitors can see how fur traders lived.

The Split Rock Lighthouse sits on a cliff on Lake Superior. Split Rock used to warn ships of the rocky shore. Today, visitors go there to learn about shipping on Lake Superior.

Duluth is the largest Minnesota city on Lake Superior. The Port of Duluth-Superior is there. It is the busiest port on the Great Lakes. Barges and freighters dock in Duluth. They come from all over the world.

North Central Minnesota

The Mesabi Iron Range is northwest of Duluth. The city of Hibbing has a huge, open-pit mine. Ironworld USA is close to Chisholm. This museum tells the history of iron mining.

Bemidji is to the west. Two famous statues stand in this town. They are of Paul Bunyan and Babe, his Blue Ox. Paul Bunyan is a lumberjack from a folktale.

Nearby is Itasca State Park. The Mississippi River begins there. Visitors only need to take a few steps to cross the river at this point. The Mississippi is less than knee-deep there.

Brainerd is south along the Mississippi. Lakes and forests are all around this town. Lumbertown USA is nearby. This is a rebuilt 1800s logging town. Buildings include a bunkhouse and mess hall.

The Twin Cities

Minneapolis and St. Paul are called the Twin Cities. Minneapolis is the state's largest city. St. Paul is the state capital.

Minneapolis has more than 20 lakes. Minnehaha Creek also flows through the city. The creek tumbles over Minnehaha Falls. Then the creek empties into the Mississippi River.

Visitors to St. Paul can board the *Jonathan Padelford* paddleboat. The Padelford travels down the Mississippi River. The trip ends at Fort Snelling.

The camp that became Fort Snelling started in 1819. Today, visitors watch actors dressed up like soldiers perform military drills. The soldiers wear uniforms from the 1800s.

Southern Minnesota

Pipestone is in far southwestern Minnesota. The town was named for a red stone. Deposits of this stone are near the town. Native Americans carved pipestone. They made pipes used in ceremonies.

Rochester is in the southeastern part of the state. This city is home to the Mayo Clinic. Doctor William W. Mayo started the clinic in 1889. His two sons, William J. and Charles, helped him. They became doctors, too. Mayo

Thief River Falls · Warroad · International Falls
Big Falls · Ely · Grand Portage
Bemidji · Chisholm · Hibbing
Moorhead · Grand Rapids · Duluth
Detroit Lakes · Crosslake
Alexandria · Brainerd
St. Cloud · St. Paul ★
Minneapolis · Red Wing
New Ulm · Northfield · Winona
Pipestone · Mankato
Luverne · Worthington · Rochester
Albert Lea

Bloomington, Brooklyn Park, Coon Rapids, Burnsville and Plymouth are suburbs of the Minneapolis and St. Paul area.

Clinic is known throughout the world for the quality of its health care.

Red Wing is northeast of Rochester. It is on the Mississippi River. This town is known for its factories that make shoes and pottery.

South of Red Wing is Lake Pepin. This is a wide spot on the Mississippi. Speed boats pull water skiers across the lake. Water skiing started there in 1922.

39

Minnesota Time Line

10,000 B.C.—The first people reach Minnesota.

A.D. 1600s—The Dakota and Ojibwa people live in Minnesota.

1679—Daniel Greysolon, sieur Duluth, arrives in present-day Duluth.

1680—Father Hennepin discovers the Falls of St. Anthony in present-day Minneapolis.

1783—The portion of Minnesota east of the Mississippi becomes United States territory.

1803—Western Minnesota becomes United States territory through the Louisiana Purchase.

1820s—Fort Snelling is built near present-day Minneapolis and St. Paul.

1832—Henry R. Schoolcraft discovers the source of the Mississippi River at Lake Itasca.

1851—The Dakota give up much of their land in Minnesota.

1858—Minnesota joins the Union as the 32nd state.

1862—The Dakota Conflict breaks out in the Minnesota River Valley.

1869—The University of Minnesota opens.

1876—The James/Younger gang tries to hold up the First National Bank in Northfield.

1889—The Mayo family founds the Mayo Clinic in Rochester.

1890—Iron ore is discovered in the Mesabi Range.

1918—The Farmer-Labor party is formed.

1944—The Farmer-Labor party joins Minnesota's Democratic party, thus forming the Democratic-Farmer-Labor party (DFL).

1963—The Guthrie Theater opens in Minneapolis.

1965—United States Senator Hubert H. Humphrey becomes vice president of the United States under Lyndon B. Johnson.

1976—United States Senator Walter Mondale is elected vice president of the United States under Jimmy Carter.

1987—The Minnesota Twins win the World Series.

1990s—Computer engineers at the University of Minnesota develop Gopher, a software program for browsing the Internet.

1991—The Minnesota Twins win the World Series.

1992—The Mall of America opens in Bloomington.

1993—Sharon Sayles Belton becomes mayor of Minneapolis and the first African-American woman mayor of a major Midwest city.

Famous Minnesotans

Charlie Bender (1883-1954) Ojibwa baseball pitcher elected to Baseball Hall of Fame in 1951; born on the White Earth Indian Reservation.

Patty Berg (1918-) Golfer who won the first U.S. Women's Open Championship in 1946 and 82 other tournaments between 1935 and 1981; born in Minneapolis.

Robert Bly (1926-) Influential poet of the 20th century; born in Madison.

William O. Douglass (1898-1980) Longest-serving U.S. Supreme Court Justice (1939-1975); born in Maine.

Bob Dylan (1941-) Singer/songwriter whose songs include "Blowin' in the Wind"; born in Duluth.

F. Scott Fitzgerald (1896-1940) Writer whose novels deal with wealthy people in the 1920s; born in St. Paul.

Wanda Gág (1893-1946) Children's author and illustrator who is best known for *Millions of Cats*; born in New Ulm.

Judy Garland (1922-1969) Actress and singer who played Dorothy in *The Wizard of Oz*; born in Grand Rapids.

Hubert H. Humphrey (1911-1978) Mayor of Minneapolis (1945-1948), U.S. senator from Minnesota (1949-1965 and 1971-1978), and vice president of the United States (1965-1969).

Charles A. Lindbergh (1902-1974) First aviator to fly solo, nonstop across the Atlantic Ocean; grew up in Little Falls.

Prince Rogers Nelson (1958-) Singer and musician; born in Minneapolis.

Alan Page (1945-) Football star with the Minnesota Vikings; became the first African-American to serve on Minnesota's Supreme Court in 1992.

Kirby Puckett (1961-) Fielder for Minnesota Twins (1984-1996); led Twins to two World Series championships (1987 and 1991).

Winona Ryder (1971-) Actress in such movies as *Little Women*; born in Winona.

Charles Schulz (1922-) Artist who created the Peanuts comic strip; born in Minneapolis.

Anne Tyler (1941-) Best-selling novelist who wrote *The Accidental Tourist*; born in Minneapolis.

August Wilson (1945-) Playwright whose plays *Fences* and *The Piano Lesson* won Pulitzer Prizes in drama; founded the Black Horizons Theater Company in St. Paul.

Words to Know

blizzard—a strong windstorm with blowing snow

casino—a place for gambling

continental United States—the 48 states not including Alaska and Hawaii

ethnic group—people who are connected by a common culture

glacier—a huge sheet of slowly moving ice

humid—air that is heavy with moisture

immigrant—a person who comes to another country to settle

museum—a place where interesting or valuable objects are displayed

population—the number of people living in a place

posse—a group of citizens usually organized by a sheriff to help catch a criminal

reservation—land set aside for use by Native Americans

tornado—a powerful windstorm that comes with a whirling, funnel-shaped cloud

tourism—the business that provides services such as lodging and food to travelers

voyageur—a person hired by a fur company to bring supplies to outposts and to take furs from the outposts

To Learn More

Aylesworth, Thomas G. and Virginia L. Aylesworth. *Western Great Lakes*. New York: Chelsea House, 1992.

Blashfield, Jean F. *Awesome Almanac: Minnesota*. Fontana, Wis.: B & B Publishing Co., 1993.

Fradin, Dennis Brindell and Judith Bloom Fradin. *Minnesota*. Sea to Shining Sea. Chicago: Children's Press, 1994.

Porter, A. P. *Minnesota*. Hello U.S.A. Minneapolis: Lerner Publications, 1992.

Stein, R. Conrad. *Minnesota*. Chicago: Children's Press, 1992.

Useful Addresses

American Swedish Institute
2600 Park Avenue South
Minneapolis, MN 55407

Grand Portage National Monument
  Headquarters
Box 666
Grand Marais, MN 55604

Itasca State Park
HCO5, Box 4
Lake Itasca, MN 56460

Mall of America
60 East Broadway
Bloomington, MN 55425

Minnesota Historical Society
345 Kellogg Boulevard West
St. Paul, MN 55102-1906

Pipestone National Monument
Box 727
Pipestone, MN 56165

Science Museum of Minnesota
30 East 10th Street
St. Paul, MN 55101

Internet Sites

City.Net Minnesota
http://city.net/countries/united_states/minnesota

Travel.org—Minnesota
http://travel.org/minnesot.html

Welcome to Minnesota
http://www.state.mn.us/welcome.html

Home of Jesse James' Defeat
http://www.northfield.org/jj

Index